SUSAN M. PE

ESKIMO CARVING

SHIRE ETHNOGRAPHY

Cover photograph
An ivory harpoon rest in the form of two polar bears, pierced for fastening, from a boat, probably an umiak; length 120 millimetres (4¾ inches). Collected by Lieutenant George Peard, RN, at Kotzebue Sound, north-west Alaska, in 1826-7.
(Photograph: Exeter City Museum, Bruce Sinclair.)

British Library Cataloguing in Publication Data available.

Published by
SHIRE PUBLICATIONS LTD
Cromwell House, Church Street, Princes Risborough,
Aylesbury, Bucks HP17 9AJ, UK

Series Editor: Bryan Cranstone

ISBN 0 85263 770 5

First published 1985

Set in 11 point Times and printed in Great Britain by
C. I. Thomas & Sons (Haverfordwest) Ltd,
Press Buildings, Merlins Bridge, Haverfordwest, Dyfed.

Contents

4

List of illustrations

Preface

The history of man in the American Arctic is long and complex, extending across some twelve millennia in time, and some 4500 miles (7200 km) in space. This book is about Eskimo carving, using the term 'Eskimo' in its loosest sense to include most of the pre-European inhabitants of eastern Siberia, northern and south-western coastal Alaska, the Canadian Arctic coast and islands, and Greenland. It concentrates, therefore, upon the last two thousand or so years of Arctic history, when people sharing in the first great exploitation of the central and eastern Arctic, known to us as the Dorset culture, and those of northern and western Alaska, who ultimately spread as the bearers of the Thule culture across to eastern Greenland, were creating powerful plastic and pictorial images.

Within this span, the Arctic people have lived according to a recognisably similar lifestyle, although one which, within the broad framework created by Arctic conditions, has differed considerably in emphasis through time and place. This common approach gives a certain underlying unity to Eskimo art, but, nevertheless, the dense engraved decoration of the Old Bering Sea ivory workers bears no close relationship to the figures of the Dorset carvers, and both are quite distinct from the present outburst of stone sculpture. Eskimo artistic history does not show a smooth line of development from an early period in the past to the present day, but rather a pattern of diverse and sporadic florescence. In this book, I have devoted most space to the most important phases of artistic creation while including enough archaeological discussion to show the historical contexts of the carvers and the relationships of the different traditions to each other. The interpretation of much Arctic archaeology and culture is controversial and I have had to simplify many issues without, it is hoped, distorting them too much.

Dating presents some problems. For dates in the pre-Christian era I have used radiocarbon dates rather than real, calendar dates. Following the usual convention these are expressed as, for example, 1000 bc rather than 1000 BC. As an approximate guide, 1000 bc represents 1200 BC and 2000 bc is equivalent to 2500 BC. It should also be noted that various spellings exist for proper names in the Arctic languages.

Susan M. Pearce

Eskimo Carving

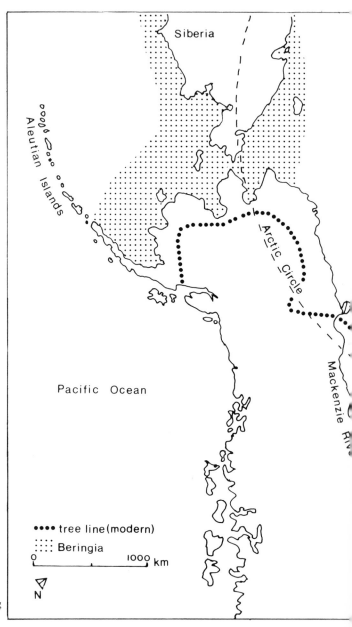

1. The Arctic, showing physical features.

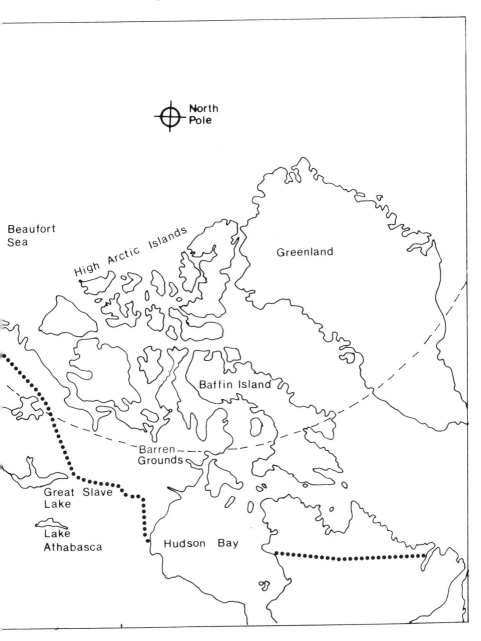

2. The Cumberland Sound, near Pangnirtung, south-east Baffin Island. The south Baffin mountains and the beginning of the Penny Ice Cap can be seen in the background. (Photograph: Susan M. Pearce.)

3. Caribou feeding on the tundra near British Petroleum/Standard Oil Company installations, Prudhoe Bay, north Alaska. (Photograph: BP Alaska.)

1
Arctic hunters and carvers

The Arctic

The Arctic of the Eskimo extends more than 4000 miles (6400 km) from the coast of eastern Greenland in the east to the fringes of Siberia in the west, northwards into the High Arctic islands, and southwards to the tip of Greenland, the west coast of Hudson Bay and Prince William Sound in Alaska (fig. 1). The Eskimo homeland lies north of the treeline (although this line has fluctuated from time to time), except where the Mackenzie River flows out into the Beaufort Sea. Much of the wood used in the Arctic originated as driftwood brought to the sea by the Mackenzie and carried eastwards by the ocean currents. The same currents bring the pack-ice from its breeding ground off the polar ice-cap eastwards through the channels of the Arctic archipelago.

The Arctic is a country of contrasts, mountainous in central Alaska and in Greenland and Baffin Island (fig. 2), with their inland ice-caps, and a flat plateau scattered with thousands of lakes in the Barren Grounds west of Hudson Bay and on the north Alaskan slope (fig. 3). In the sub-Arctic, below the Arctic Circle, the willow scrub grows densely in some places and in the spring the earth smells of wild thyme. Elsewhere, in the Barren Grounds and in the ice-bound High Arctic islands (fig. 4), the tundra, grassless with its mosses and lichens, stretches desolate to the horizon, but even here in summer the fragile yellow Arctic poppies grow straight out of the stones. In the short Arctic summer, when it is light for all or much of the time, the land is not snow-bound, but in the long winter the dark and ice close in.

For hunters with skills and positive attitudes the Arctic is not inhospitable because it abounds in food animals. For most of the Eskimo the seals are very important — the very common ringed seals and the bearded seals, both of which remain in Arctic waters all year round, breathing through holes in the winter ice, and are caught with specially developed harpooning gear (fig. 5). Migrant animals, too, are often crucial: the white (or beluga) whales, which swim into the Arctic in summer by way of well known routes; the Greenland or bowhead whales, which swim south from polar waters in the winter; and the Barren Grounds caribou, which migrate to the forest fringes as the cold returns.

4. Sea ice in the High Arctic, looking from Cornwallis Island across Barrow Strait. (Photograph: Susan M. Pearce.)

Walruses provide meat, furs and, above all, ivory, which comes from their two upper canines. These are formed of two layers of dentine, the outer of which is very dense and homogeneous and contains gelatinous material so that it can take detailed carving and a fine natural polish. Walrus tusks can be up to 650 millimetres (25½ inches) in length. Musk-oxen offer meat and hides and birds like gulls and ducks vary the diet. The polar bears, standing up to 2.5 metres (8 feet 2 inches) high on their hind legs, dangerous and beautiful in their magnificent creamy pelts, are the acknowledged lords of the Arctic ice and the focus of important imagery and art.

The people

There are today about eighty thousand Eskimo in the world, scattered across their vast area from the Russian Bering Sea coastlands to eastern Greenland. Most Eskimo call themselves (and prefer to be called) Inuit, which simply means 'men'; the word 'Eskimo' is apparently an Algonquin Indian term meaning 'raw-meat-eater', which was applied to the Arctic people first by the French in the seventeenth century, and then by the British. Physically, the Eskimo are a mongolian people, with the characteristic straight black hair, dark brown eyes, high cheek-bones and yellow-brown skin. They are not a particularly short race, although their bulky clothing has sometimes created this impression.

The Eskimo language has not yet been shown to relate to any other known language family. Its grammar is very complex and words can be modified by adding suffixes: for example *tuktoo* means 'a caribou', *tuktoojuak* 'a big caribou', *tuktoojuakseok* 'hunt a big caribou', *tuktoojuakseokniakpunga* 'I will hunt a big caribou'. Remarkably, today, as in recent historic times, an Eskimo from Greenland can make himself understood, although with some difficulty, all the way to Bering Strait. Across this huge area Eastern Eskimo, or Inupik, one branch of the Eskimo language family, is spoken, but in the west there are two other branches not intelligible either to each other or to the northern and eastern Eskimo: western Eskimo, or Yupik, on the Alaskan south-western coastlands and in Siberia; and Aleutian in the

5. Harpoon head of developed form, with a range of characteristic elements. The design of these elements differs through time, and they may be absent altogether, features which are of great importance in the dating of harpoon heads and so of archaeological deposits. (After Bandi 1969, 12.)

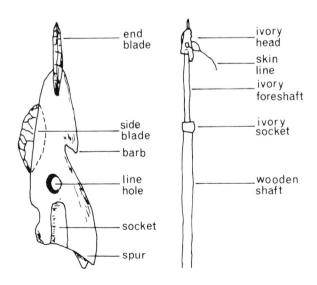

end blade

side blade

barb

line hole

socket

spur

ivory head

skin line

ivory foreshaft

ivory socket

wooden shaft

Aleutian Islands. Some philologists believe that Aleutian and Eskimoan, or Inupik-Yupik, diverged from a common ancestor, Eskaleutian, about four thousand years ago, and that Inupik and Yupik separated about a thousand years ago.

Archaeologists generally now believe that most of the ancestors of all the Eskimo-Aleut groups came directly from neighbouring Siberia, but this may have involved more than one episode of migration. People of the Palaeo-arctic tradition, who possessed small, specialised stone tools and larger cutting blades, seem to have reached Alaska during the closing stages of the Bering Land Bridge, sometimes called Beringia (created when the sea level was lowered because much water was locked up as ice during the final ice age), around 10,000 bc, but the further Arctic remained uninhabited.

Around 5000 bc warmer conditions, known as the Thermal Maximum, seem to have encouraged some groups from the southern interior of North America, whose lanceolate and side-notched stone projectile points are described as the Northern Arctic tradition, to move into Alaska. These proto-American Indians do not seem to have been closely involved in the development of later Eskimo groups but their relation with the people of the Palaeo-arctic tradition is clearly complicated. Along the Alaskan Pacific coast and in the Aleutian Islands cultural developments seem to have progressed from this basis, undisturbed by major outside contacts until AD 1000.

It was not until around 2000 bc that groups with tool kits drawn from Palaeo-arctic traditions spread rapidly across northern Alaska and eastward over the tundra and the Arctic islands and coastlands, a process which, conceivably, is reflected in the history of the Eskimo language family. Their tools included exquisitely worked microblades, probably used as spear and arrow points, scrapers and adzes, and they may have worn tailored skin clothing. These people were developing abilities to exploit the Arctic animals and were probably newly arrived from Siberia but perhaps partly drawn from existing settlers. Their culture is known as the Arctic Small Tool tradition, and they created a thin veneer of Arctic occupation, adapting themselves to the local food resources.

The hunters' lifestyle

European accounts tell us much about nineteenth-century and early twentieth-century Eskimo communities and, used carefully, can help us to understand the lifestyles of earlier Arctic groups.

6. Eskimo pulling meat on sleds, Pelly Bay, central Arctic. (Photograph: Information Canada Photothèque, John Reeves, March 1968.)

Of fundamental importance was the maintenance of a balance between the hunting community and the food animals in its territory. For this reason a group perhaps numbered around fifty to seventy people and growth may sometimes have been checked by the exposure of infants and the suicide of the elderly. The group was of one blood kin although strangers of either sex were sometimes received in, and the offspring of all unions were accepted as children of the community.

Authority was vested not in any institution but in individuals who impressed the rest with their sagacity and prowess. The use of property, including houses and stored food, was normally shared among the group (fig. 6), although men would have had their own hunting gear and women their own sewing kit, meat and warm waterproof clothing being equally crucial to survival. Many Eskimo groups have built themselves substantial home settlements, which served as their hunting base through most of the year and offered secure leisure during the dark days of winter for carving, story telling and dancing by the light of the seal-oil lamps, sometimes in a permanent house, sometimes in a specially constructed snow house (fig. 9). In the summer many groups

brought out their skin tents and moved to a traditional coastal or
estuarine spot to take advantage of migrating whales or the
seasonal runs of Arctic char, a fish which makes excellent eating
raw and cooked (fig. 7).

The Eskimo groups have developed a large number of tools
and techniques for the working of walrus ivory, bone, antler and
wood. Before carving, the animal materials are usually soaked in
urine to soften them and may be wetted with urine as the work
progresses. Before contact with European civilisation, virtually
all tools were made of chipped stone, but since about 1800 these
have been gradually replaced by metal blades. Axes or adzes are
used to rough out large wooden or bone objects, but for all
detailed work, and for ivory carving, the knife is the principal
tool, with its 80 or 100 millimetre (3-4 inch) blade, sometimes
curved, set in a wooden or horn handle which tapers to a point.

Chisels, sometimes made of beaver tooth, are used, and pieces
are finished with antler polishers, cut with notches so that angles
can be smoothed. Bow drills are used for piercing holes and for
some engraving work; the wooden drill with its point is made to

7. Eskimo looking out to sea, standing beside sealskin tent and kayak, Pelly Bay, central
Arctic. (Photograph: Information Canada Phototèque, D. Wilkinson, 1961.)

8. Ivory carver using bow drill, Point Barrow, north Alaska. (Photograph: T. P. Brower.)

revolve rapidly by means of a rawhide thong passed twice around it and fastened to a bow at each end. The bow is sawn backwards and forwards and the drill is often held in the teeth (fig. 8). The black paint sometimes used to pick out engravings is made from plumbago, charcoal or gunpowder, the last two mixed with blood. Red is obtained from iron oxide, green from copper oxide and yellow from a range of ochres. Tools and carvings in progress are kept in wooden boxes, or in skin satchels with arched bone or ivory handles.

The shaman

Like most non-European peoples, the Eskimo do not have a word for 'art', which they conceive as the natural expression of the world of men and spirits, and this makes the shaman a significant figure.

Men find their shamanistic vocation as adolescents, and its validity is confirmed for the individual and the group through the visionary experiences which the shaman undergoes, induced by a well recognised range of techniques, like self-deprivation of food, warmth and sleep, hypnotism and drug use, which are passed from one shaman to another. Shamans describe terrifying journeys through cold countrysides assisted by animal helpers whom they meet, and it is sometimes difficult to tell whether these regions are conceived as spirit lands with an external

9. Drum dance in a snow house, Christmas 1962, Pelly Bay, central Arctic. (Photograph: Information Canada Photothèque, D. Wilkinson, 1962.)

existence, or whether they are recognised as journeys into the shaman's own psyche. Shamans also think themselves into the hard and soft parts of their own bodies, achieving a rapport between mind, blood and organs that embraces the hunter and the hunted and that touches profound human emotions.

Shamans are imaginative, creative people, and among many, although perhaps not all, Eskimo communities, their perceptions have been the inspiration behind the carvings, which they may produce themselves, or in co-operation with the carver. They may also have tendencies which European society might call 'disturbed' and, perhaps, minority sexual tastes (shamans sometimes wear items of women's clothing) and Eskimo society provides an honoured place for individuals with all these characteristics who give outward expression to tensions within the group.

The shaman is the group's link with the other world and, as such, he is consulted in times of sickness or of scarcity, when his séance contact with the spirits may mingle with other forms of hunting magic. He also plays a central part in the annual festivals, which seem to be typical of Eskimo life. At all these times he employs a repertoire which includes ventriloquism, sleight of hand, hypnosis and utterances from trance-like states, stimulated by smoke, bizarre clothing from which hang sacred objects, masks sometimes, and, above all, the throbbing beat of the single-sided drum (fig. 9). Shamans act within the tradition of ecstatic religion which seems to be a part of the inheritance of all the circumpolar peoples and which may reach back into the palaeolithic past. In spite of its trickery, its strength lies in its genuine pyschological insights into the nature and needs of men, especially those in a hunting band, and this ensures the mutual confidence between a shaman and his community.

Eskimo Carving

10. The eastern Arctic, showing places mentioned in the text.

2
The classic sculptors of the central Arctic

The emergence of the Dorset lifestyle

In the central Arctic basin, bounded by the northern shores of Hudson Bay, Hudson Strait and western Baffin Island, and on the neighbouring Arctic coasts, the Small Tool makers had established themselves soon after 2000 bc, setting up their camps on the coasts, hunting the sea mammals and the caribou, fishing, and knapping their superb stone tools (fig. 10). At Igloolik Island, off Melville Peninsula, have been found the remains of their camps, marked by the rings of stones which once held down their skin tents and the central slabs where once their fires were built.

Soon after 1500 bc climatic changes in Arctic Canada forced this way of life to change. The climate deteriorated, bringing harder winters and cooler summers, which permitted the growth of thicker and more extensive sea ice, and which, in turn, made the sea mammals less accessible. In the Barren Grounds the treeline retreated south by more than 200 kilometres (125 miles), a process apparently complicated by a series of disastrous forest fires, and this in turn affected the migration routes of the caribou. The Small Tool makers, whose traditional camping and hunting patterns were now inadequate, adopted various new approaches. Some areas were abandoned, especially the north coast of Greenland and the High Arctic islands north of Lancaster Sound. Some hunters moved into the interior of the Barren Grounds, as far south perhaps as Great Slave Lake and Lake Athabasca, competing with the traditional Indian occupants for the caribou. In the central Arctic basin, however, new and satisfactory lifestyles were developed.

Settlements became considerably larger and much more permanent. In some areas they included rectangular semi-subterranean winter houses with turf walls, strengthened with stone and covered with sewn skins. Inside these were small stone-slab hearths and, along the walls, sod-built benches for sitting and sleeping. The settlements often had a larger meeting house. In other places the people built domed snow houses,

heated with blubber-oil lamps carved from soapstone. Both must
have been much more comfortable in the winter than the earlier
skin tents warmed by small fires of bones and driftwood, and
tents were now used only in the summer. There is some evidence
that they possessed kayaks, possibly an Alaskan invention,
knowledge of which had presumably travelled east along the
seaways. They seem to have used sleds, although these were
drawn by hand, not by dogs, and bone ice creepers were fastened
to the feet to improve travel over snow. They possessed the usual
range of small stone tools, together with the bone harpoon head
pierced to take a line, and they probably sewed close-fitting fur
clothing. Refuse around their settlements shows that they were
effective hunters of the seals and walruses, and also, in some
places, of the caribou herds.

   Together, these new approaches made possible a more secure,
settled way of life, even though conditions on the tundra and the
coasts were becoming increasingly severe. They are known as the
Dorset culture, and their possessors as the Dorset people,
because they were first recognised archaeologically at Cape
Dorset on south-west Baffin Island. During the centuries after
800 bc Dorset people spread back into the High Arctic islands for
a time, and down the coast of Labrador as far as Newfoundland,
and perhaps as far west as Amundsen Gulf. The new security,
and the confidence which it brought, inspired the development of
a major art style.

Dorset ivory sculptures

   The characteristic approach employed by the Dorset sculptors
was of three-dimensional figure carving in the round, usually of
ivory, but sometimes of bone or wood, and of a size small enough
to hold comfortably in the hand. In contrast to most other Arctic
art, dating from before European contact, line decoration and
patterning were very seldom used, either on the figure sculptures
or on domestic and hunting implements. As in all art, form and
content are inextricably interwoven, and the small size of the
pieces does not detract from their great vitality; they exude
intensity and power, whether the finished concept is realistic or
highly stylised. Dorset carvings are relatively rare, and probably
no more than a few hundred are known altogether. This,
combined with the high technical qualities which they show and
the clear sense they give of a coherent aesthetic tradition,
suggests that Dorset art was not the product of widespread,

11. Ivory maskette excavated at Dorset site, Tyara, Sugluk, Arctic Quebec; height 35 millimetres (1⅜ inches). (Photograph: Canadian Eskimo Arts Council.)

general activity among the communities but rather was created by specialists able to articulate concepts about their carvings and to pass their traditions on.

An analysis of Dorset subjects suggests that about a third are concerned with human depictions (figurines, part figurines, faces and maskettes) (fig. 11), about a fifth show bears, about another third show seals, walruses and birds, and the rest are concerned with caribou, fish and small animals like weasels. Clearly the carvers were chiefly interested in people, bears and sea mammals, while they were not at all concerned to depict insects, plants or structures. The ideas behind the carving must be reflected in the choice of subject matter.

A number of the pieces showing seabirds, caribou or walruses, often represented only by a hoof or a head, are pierced with holes for hanging and were presumably worn around the neck or, conceivably, sewn on to clothing. It is likely that these embodied hunting magic, intended to bring the hunter success and forgiveness from the animals which he killed, and sympathetic magic, intended to endow him with the cunning of the weasel, the swiftness of the caribou, and so on. Some of the human depictions, full of controlled force as they are, may have stemmed from similar ideas of luck and power, although they are

12. *(left)* Ivory figurine, excavated in 1939 from Dorset site at Abverdjar, near Igloolik, central Arctic; height 50 millimetres (2 inches). (Photograph: University Museum of Archaeology and Anthropology, Cambridge.)

13. *(below)* Ivory miniature polar bear heads, bear and two upright bears, from the Dorset site at Abverdjar, near Igloolik, central Arctic; height of largest 65 millimetres (2½ inches). The heads are finished with a clean cut below the neck but holes at the back suggest that they were meant to be hung up or sewn on clothing. The upright bears show skeletal marking. (Photograph: University Museum of Archaeology and Anthropology, Cambridge.)

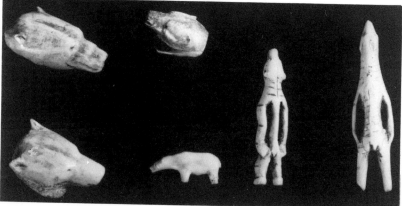

sometimes difficult to interpret; does the carving in figure 12 represent a trial of strength between two men, or is it a father carrying his son on his shoulders? The small amulets, and perhaps some of the human figures, are likely to be personal possessions with purely magical properties.

Bear figurines

The bear figurines and some of the other animal pieces, on the other hand, have characteristics which suggest that they were part of the equipment of Dorset shamans. Much later European accounts show that bears were often the shaman's greatest helping spirit, who gave him power and led him to other helpers who assisted his spirit in its great flights over land and sea and ice. The shaman's relationship with these animal spirits, who often appeared in human form, was a delicate balance of dependence and control, fraught with dangers and tensions, and the spirits may have been embodied in the bear carvings, and sometimes the bird carvings, which perhaps the shaman kept in special bags hanging from his neck or his clothing (fig. 13).

Bear figurines are characteristically carved with the outline of the skeleton, and perhaps some of the internal organs, shown on the outside, as if the backbone, ribs and joints had been projected outwards, rendering the animal down through blood and flesh to its essentials (fig. 14). The skeletal motif in bear sculpture seems

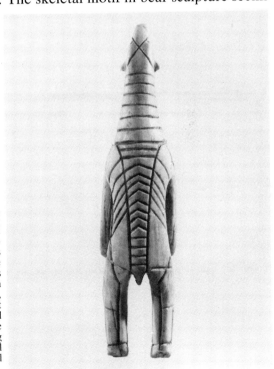

14. Ivory polar bear figurine, from the Dorset site at Alarnerk near Igloolik, central Arctic; height 157 millimetres (6¼ inches). This splendid bear carries the skeletal motif, and its joints and head are marked with crosses. The body is hollow, and at the back of the throat is a cavity in which was found red ochre. This cavity can be closed by means of a sliding lid. (Photograph: National Museum of Man, National Museums of Canada.)

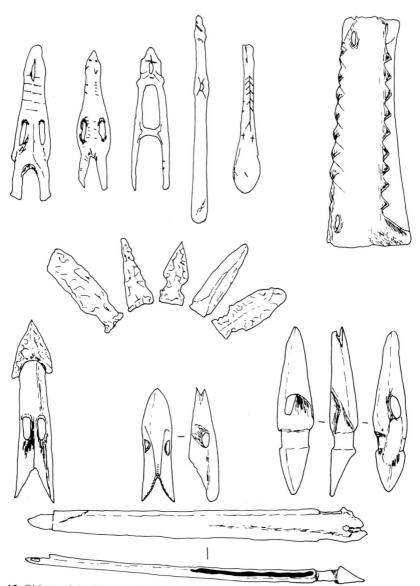

15. Objects of the Dorset culture from various Dorset sites in Arctic Canada. Five bear forms showing increasing stylisation (above left); length of longest 76 millimetres (3 inches). (After Meldgaard 1960, plate II.) Ice creeper of antler meant to be lashed to the foot (above right); length 125 millimetres (4⅞ inches). Five chipped stone implements (centre), a side-notched knife and four projectiles; length of knife 48 millimetres (1⅞ inches). Three harpoon heads and a cloven-footed lance (below) which would have carried an end blade and two side blades; length of longest harpoon head 80 millimetres (3⅛ inches); length of lance 200 millimetres (7⅞ inches). (All after Dumond 1977, 94, 96.)

to have begun fairly early in the Dorset culture and to have continued to its end, perhaps gradually becoming increasingly stylised until only a spatula-shaped object was created, still marked with backbone, liver and heart (fig. 15). Some Dorset bears carry crosses, or Xs, at joints and neck, perhaps to emphasise important and vulnerable places. We have noted that, just as the shaman took long spirit journeys across the country, so he took them into himself. He encouraged the appearance of the helping spirits by mentally divesting his body of its flesh and blood, seeing himself as a skeleton, and naming every bone and organ in the sacred shaman's language, so that his skeleton, the longest-lasting part of his body, was dedicated to his task.

The skeletal bear carvings fit very well into these ideas and, like much of the Dorset art, may well have been created by shaman master carvers.

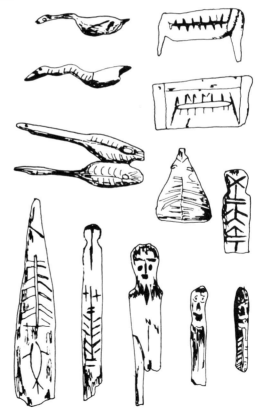

16. Dorset culture pieces. Ivory swans (top left), Mansel Island; length of longest 60 millimetres (2⅜ inches). Ivory shaman's teeth (top right), from Alarnerk site, Igloolik (upper) and Button Point (lower); length 45 millimetres (1¾ inches). Wooden figurines of bear forms and human forms (bottom) showing slits cut in the body, from Button Point, Baffin Island; length of longest about 100 millimetres (4 inches). (After Taylor and Swinton 1967, 10, 11, 18.)

Shamans' equipment

Many of the ivory bear carvings have a deep groove or longitudinal slit in their backs, occasionally enclosed by a sliding cover, and sometimes filled or marked with red ochre, presumably representing blood. The rare find of wooden carvings at Button Point, on north-east Baffin Island, which helps to fill out the picture offered by the occasional wooden finds made in Greenland, Victoria Island and around Lake Harbour, and which is probably our best representative of an important aspect of Dorset art, contained two probable bear carvings with this slit, and seal and large fish carvings similarly cut. The slits seem originally to have held slivers of wood, for in two of them the slivers remained in position. More sinister are three Button Point armless human busts, a human doll with separate arms and legs and two abstract human figures: these had a slot cut in the throat or the upper chest, and in two the wooden sliver was still embedded. Some of these pieces, also, showed traces of red ochre stain. It is difficult not to believe that these figures represent animals and men 'killed', or spirits emptied and subdued, by the shaman, who must have carved and stabbed them (fig. 16).

The Button Point find also contained pieces of shamans' equipment, including the probable fragment of a drum rim and two fragments of life-size wooden face masks. In masks like these may have been set the ivory shamans' teeth, known from Dorset contexts (fig. 16), and they may have been worn for shamanistic rituals or for shamans' burials, the mask serving to seal off from the community the dangers of the dead shaman. Containers made from the end of a walrus tusk, characterised by stylised human

17. Caribou antler carved with human faces, excavated from the Dorset site at Abverdjar, near Igloolik, central Arctic, in 1939; length 201 millimetres (8 inches). (Photograph: University Museum of Archaeology and Anthropology, Cambridge.)

faces, walrus-head motifs and the significant crosses, are probably shamans' utensil cases. Ivory tubes, bearing again animal
heads and crosses, may well be shamans' sucking tubes for
catching the breathing spirit.

Different from these carvings are the rare finds of caribou
antler, or occasionally ivory, especially from the Igloolik area,
which are densely carved with massed clusters of human faces
(fig. 17). Similar in design, but on a larger scale, are the multiple
depictions of human faces cut into the surfaces of soapstone
outcrops in the Wakeham Bay region on the south side of Hudson
Strait. These petroglyph sites must presumably have marked
areas of special significance to the Dorset people: we can only
guess that they had something to do with burials and that the
soapstone faces, like perhaps those on the antlers, represent the
dead.

The origins and connections of Dorset art

Carvings occur throughout the Dorset culture, but there seems
to have been a great increase in both numbers and variety during
the last centuries of the Dorset period, between about AD 500
and 1000. This is what we would expect, because it coincides with
the maximum Dorset expansion to the west and south and reflects
a time of security and prosperity in which mature communities in
good balance with their environment had the capacity to cultivate
religion and art.

Much has been written about the supposed cultural links and
debts of Dorset sculpture. The preceding Small Tool people seem
to have had little that can be called art and nothing that could
have inspired the Dorset flowering, and so some scholars have
looked for its inspiration to the Indians of the southern
woodlands and, especially for the later stages of Dorset art, to the
broadly contemporary Ipiutak tradition to the west (see chapter
3), with which, although the general parallels in style, form and
technique are thin, Dorset does share some concepts, including
shamans' face masks and the skeletal motif on animal figures.
Only archaeology, itself in some confusion over the relative
merits of cultural diffusion and independent development, will be
able to shed more light on these difficult problems. Perhaps
future work will demonstrate specific east-west links; perhaps it
will show that common ideas, particularly in religion and so in its
artistic expression, draw on a stock which was common to all the
Arctic people (and perhaps some of the northern Indians as well)
from their Palaeo-arctic ancestors.

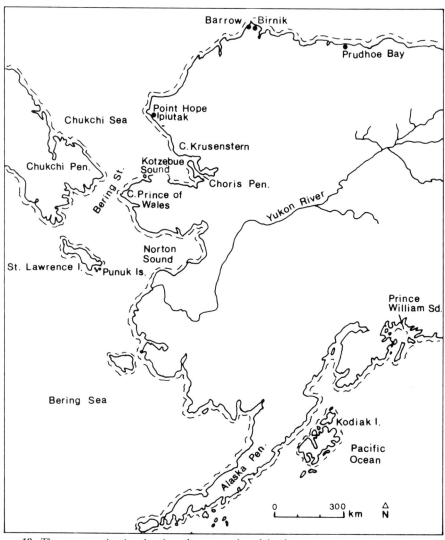

18. The western Arctic, showing places mentioned in the text.

3
The early carvers of the far west

Cultural developments

In the eastern Arctic a steady cultural development appears in which the Small Tool tradition matured into the stable Dorset tradition. In Alaska, north of the Alaskan peninsula, the cultural pattern is more complex but it has given us some of the richest Eskimo carving (fig. 18). Throughout Alaska, around 1500 bc the Small Tool tradition seems to have ceased abruptly, probably as a result of fluctuations in climate, but in the north this disappearance was followed quite quickly by the appearance of various groups whose traditions shared in Small Tool ancestry but who also possessed some distinctively Siberian equipment, particularly pottery.

This broad tradition is often called Palaeo-eskimo, and it includes the material assemblages usually called Choris, which runs down to around 500 bc, and Norton, which followed and persisted well into the Christian era. The Norton tradition included projectile points of crude appearance, polished slate implements, oil lamps and other stone vessels, harpoon heads with toggles, pottery and solid, square, permanent houses, which included *kazigi,* the combined ceremonial house and men's residence. In north-west Alaska, sites at Cape Krusenstern, at Derring on the Seward Peninsula and, above all, at Ipiutak near Point Hope show the development of a late variant of the Norton tradition of particular social and artistic complexity, beginning perhaps around AD 1 and persisting as late as AD 800 in some places.

Further south, in the coastlands and islands of the Bering Sea, there was developing a way of life probably based upon Norton traditions, but now orientated almost entirely to subsistence upon the sea mammals. These Bering Sea people possessed fully developed toggle harpoons for sealing and walrus hunting, and they probably caught some whales. They had kayaks, hand-pulled sleds, fish spears, bird-hunting gear, flint arrowheads and scrapers, and a range of ground slate tools, including the crescent-shaped women's knives, or *ulus,* for working skins. They made a variety of household goods from bone and ivory, and they produced crude pottery cooking pots and lamps. Their figurines suggest that they wore the typical Eskimo trousers and *parkas,* or hooded close-fitting jackets, and that they tattooed their faces. They seem to have constructed rectangular houses with entrance passages.

Within this Bering Sea tradition two important art styles can be distinguished, known as Okvik and Old Bering Sea. Okvik has often been regarded as the earlier, and its date has sometimes been placed very early indeed, long before the beginning of the Christian era. Fresh radiocarbon dating evidence, however, suggests that the two styles are broadly contemporary, although Okvik may have begun a little earlier, and that both flourished between about AD 1 and AD 500, so that they parallel Ipiutak art further north.

In the Bering Sea area the Punuk stage of development followed from around AD 500, showing an expanded range of sea-mammal hunting gear, including that for hunting whales, and the solid, semi-subterranean, square or rectangular whalebone, driftwood and turf houses, equipped with entrance passages to preserve warmth, which were to be built in the area until the nineteenth century AD. Further north, around the Chukchi Sea, similar developments take their name from the type site at Birnik. The unified tradition which begins with developments around the Bering Sea and continues into the Punuk and Birnik stages shows a pattern of evolution which stresses the maritime resources and becomes steadily more dependent upon an ability to catch whales. This may probably be regarded as the early phases of the great Thule tradition, which, in its maturity, would come to dominate the Arctic peoples.

Life and death at Ipiutak

The site at Ipiutak, near Point Hope on the north-west Alaskan coast, discovered in 1939, remains the most remarkable and in some ways the most enigmatic site ever found in the Arctic (fig. 19). The Ipiutak settlement comprised a large village of more than six hundred houses, each semi-subterranean, rectangular and usually measuring 4 by 5 metres (13 by 16 feet), log-built, with central hearths and side benches, arranged in five rough rows across a strip formed by beach ridges. Estimates of the length of time during which the settlement, or the individual houses, were occupied, and so of the population size, have differed considerably, but most archaeologists believe that occupation centred around AD 350. It is also possible that the

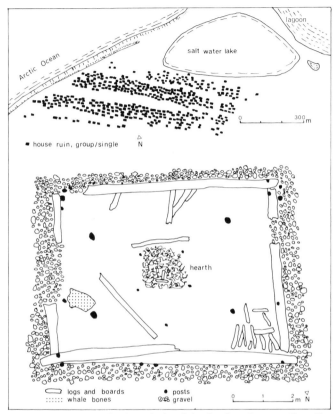

19. Plan of the settlement at Ipiutak, and of an Ipiutak culture house at Cape Krusenstern, Alaska. (After Bandi 1969, 101, 116.)

village was used only as winter quarters and that the Ipiutak people spent their summers in the interior.

Food remains suggest that sealing was very important to the Ipiutak people, although they also hunted caribou with bows, and probably some whales. They were familiar with kayaks and sleds and used a limited range of ground slate tools and well-worked flint projectile points and scrapers. They had a range of birch-bark containers, made from material acquired from further south, and these took the place of pottery cooking pots or blubber lamps.

The unique interest of Ipiutak, however, is concentrated in its graveyard, east of the houses, where some 140 graves have been investigated and have yielded an amazing collection of carved ivory objects. In many graves, the dead were interred in a log driftwood coffin, usually lying extended and usually singly, although some coffins had three skeletons. The skulls of some of the skeletons had artificial ivory eyeballs with jade pupils placed in the eye sockets from which the eyes had been gouged, and one of these skulls also had two ivory nose-plugs which end in bird-like heads inlaid with eyes of jade. Three other burials had ivory carvings representing lips sewn together. All these pieces seem to reflect a belief that the body openings of the dead must be sealed, either to protect the body against disturbances from evil spirits, or to contain the spirit of the dead which might endanger the living.

Several of the bodies had masks, which were apparently intended to perform the same function in a more elaborate form. The simplest consisted of antler plates covering the dead face. There were also three ivory masks, made up of flat sections of ivory neatly fitted together to form the outline of a human or human-animal face. They had evidently been mounted on

20. Mask of seven pieces of ivory including a separate nose, from an Ipiutak grave at the Point Hope settlement, north Alaska; height 164 millimetres (6½ inches). The pieces have stylised animal heads carved in relief. Under the mouth two large pieces of jade have been inserted as labrets (decorative plugs worn in the area into historic times) and some eighty cavities have been inlaid with jade. Fragments of a second mask (below), and related ornaments. (Photograph: American Museum of Natural History.)

21. Ivory figurine of young walrus (above); length 75 millimetres (3 inches). Openwork carving of loon (centre). Two arrowheads and a human maskette (bottom left). Openwork carvings (bottom right) and chain (right). Ipiutak; length of chain 250 millimetres (9⅞ inches). (After Bandi 1969, 112, 115.)

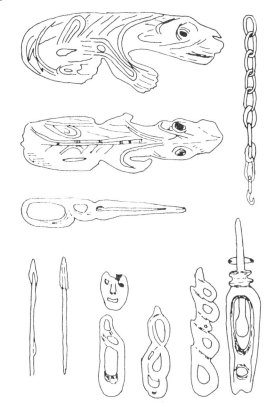

wooden backgrounds, of which few traces remained. One of the two most elaborate masks was found on the chest of a child in a burial that also contained a man and a woman: it had four outer parts, with sewn-together mouth, eyebrows, a centre piece for the nose and two jade pieces which were probably eye pupils, and the set also included two large labrets and various jade inlays and ivory pendants. The second elaborate mask comprises seven individual pieces, held together by cleats (fig. 20).

The coffin burials, and sometimes the house ruins too, have also yielded some animal carvings, many of them in naturalistic styles. These include images of polar bears and seals, and less frequently of walruses and wolves, although the finest of all is of a young walrus which, like some of the other figurines, carries the 'skeletal motif', the stylised representation of the spine with the ribs attached, shown on the animal's surface, which, as we have seen, was important in Dorset art (fig. 21).

The Ipiutak repertoire did not end here. A special group of burials had been placed directly on, or just under, the sod, perhaps covered by a log pile or enclosed in a log frame, so that the corpse had been exposed or semi-exposed until the bones sank into the ground once the flesh had completely decomposed. These surface burials were accompanied by carvings of a special type known as 'openwork carvings', of which some two hundred have been found, no two of which are identical (fig. 21). These comprise three separate elements: fantastic animal figures, swivels, and chains. The openwork animals often cannot be identified, although some are certainly carved in the form of the head of a loon (a northern diving bird), and one of the coffin burials with ivory eyeballs also had the skull of a loon equipped with similar ivory eyes. Swivels served practical purposes with dog harness and harpoon lines, but the examples with the burials, judging by their size and decoration, seem to have had symbolic intention. Chains are known throughout the Eskimo area but are especially common at Ipiutak. All the openwork carvings achieve a high level of technical skill.

The openwork carvings, and the surface burials which they accompany, presumably belonged to a specialised group within the community, and these are likely to have been the shamans. The carvings themselves may well have been created by shamans and used as part of their regalia, sewn to their skin garments. The skeletal motif employed on some of the figurines fits in with shamanistic concepts, and so does the carving of the loon, who held a special place in the mythology of the whole northern world throughout America and Asia. The loon was the earth-diver who brought up pieces of the primordial ocean bottom to form the world. He was also an important animal helper who conducted the shaman on his journeys to the underworld, and figurines of loons were set up over Siberian shamans' graves. Loons were also associated with the curing of blindness, both spiritual and physical, and the burial which included the skeletons of a man and a loon, both equipped with artificial eyes, may show us the bird as a bringer of everlasting vision in the world below. The coffin burials may also have been of shamans, or of the important members of the community.

Cultural links have often been claimed between Ipiutak and north-east Asia. The mythical importance of the loon in both areas has already been noted, and in both areas shamans seem to have sewn carvings on to their clothes, ivory in Alaska, iron in Asia. The Ipiutak burial masks are strikingly similar to the 'demon masks' found in graves at An-yang, the Shang capital in northern China. All these resemblances could have arisen from a pool of religious ideas centring upon the shaman, which were common to the circumpolar people, and which were brought to artistic flowering in specially favoured times and places.

Okvik sculptors

Okvik is a site on the Punuk Islands off the east end of St Lawrence Island, where characteristic material of this style was first discovered in 1931. St Lawrence Island has always had cultural connections with the Asiatic side of the Bering Sea, and Okvik-style artwork has been found mostly on this western side, apart from scattered finds in west Alaska. Okvik ivory harpoons and other implements are engraved with ornamental motifs, which include spurred lines, Y figures, circles, lines and ladder-like designs, combined in patterns. Some scholars divide these

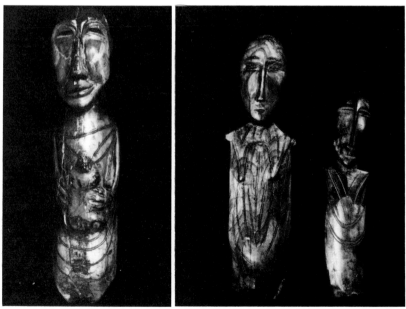

22. *(left)* Ivory female figurine, the 'Okvik Madonna' excavated in 1944 from the Punuk Islands, near St Lawrence Island, Bering Sea; height 167 millimetres (6½ inches). The small figure being carried is damaged. (Photograph: University of Alaska Museum.)
23. *(right)* Ivory female figurine (left), discovered in 1972 on St Lawrence Island, Bering Sea; height 200 millimetres (7⅞ inches). Ivory figurine with stylised head and torso (right), found on Punuk Islands, near St Lawrence Island, Bering Sea; height 156 millimetres (6⅛ inches). (Photograph: Alaska State Museum, Alfred A. Blaker.)

24. Ivory standing figure, Okvik period, Alaska; height 165 millimetres (6½ inches). The head is round rather than ovoid, the pregnant body is realistically squat and the style is more naturalistic than most other known Okvik figurines, but the figure does not fit into any later phase of Alaskan Eskimo art. (Photograph: Robert and Lisa Sainsbury Collection, University of East Anglia.)

into three chronological phases, beginning with sub-style A, where the decoration consists chiefly of deeply cut, thick, straight or slightly curved lines, to which side spurs were attached. Sub-style B, a more delicate style, included short slanting lines making up a tent-like figure, line and spur combinations, small circles with central dots, and plug inlays representing eyes. Sub-style C, the most elaborate, was characterised by a profusion of carefully spurred lines, often in pairs, and often arranged to converge upon a small circle. Some of the line groups on the harpoons may be the equivalent of the tattooed lines on human faces, and both will have carried powerful magic.

The glory of Okvik sculptural art rests in its ivory figurines, among which human forms, usually female, predominate, and animal figures, often of fantastic form, of whales, seals, walruses, bears and dogs, are less common. Decoration on these figures sometimes makes it possible to tie them in chronologically with the artistic sub-styles. Forty-five human figures were found at the site on the Punuk Islands, all characterised by a stylised form of face and head, the head pointed, the face long and oval with a narrow pointed chin and long straight nose. The body shape is usually only indicated. The most famous of the ivory figurines is the 'Okvik Madonna', showing a woman with a finely sculptured face and a twisted smile holding in her arms a child or, more probably, a bear cub or a dog (fig. 22). Equally impressive is a similar figurine more recently discovered at St Lawrence Island, which has the same sensitivity of expression in the face, the shoulders and the breasts, but which seems to be pregnant (fig. 23). Both figures are engraved with gently curved lines evocative of flowing garments. More chilling is another female figure from the Punuk Islands, which has a similar face, breasts represented by concentric circles, and incised lines and circles over the body area, but also fully realised, short, bowed legs ending in bear's paws, exaggerated hips and gaping, oversized genitals.

The Okvik figurines had, presumably, a religious significance for their carvers, and the predominance of female forms,

25. Ivory carvings from Old Bering Sea culture: (left) harpoon head; (centre) gorget or pectoral, engraved in Old Bering Sea Style II; (above) 'winged object'; (right) harpoon head; (below) ? pendant, in Old Bering Sea Style III. Length of winged object 165 millimetres (6½ inches). (Photograph: Smithsonian Institution.)

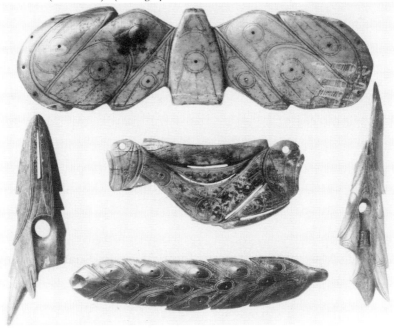

sometimes with animal traits, some apparently benign and others terrifying, suggests that this centred upon a Lady of the Animals who commanded the fertility of men and food beasts, reminiscent perhaps of earlier palaeolithic female deities in the Old World (fig. 24). The human and animal carvings are likely to have figured in magic hunting rituals, perhaps presided over by the shamans, to whose clothing some of the smaller ivory animals and masks seem to have been attached and who may already have been using the single-sided drum.

Old Bering Sea engravers
Old Bering Sea art is essentially that of the ivory engraver, and line decoration was applied to harpoon heads, and to almost every piece which was capable of taking it — harpoon foreshafts, snow goggles, needle cases, hooks, toggles and ornaments. Art historians have distinguished three phases in this decoration, which have proved to be of great importance in the dating of the harpoon-head sequence.

Old Bering Sea I concentrates upon lines, spurs, elipses and circles (roughly AD 1 to 100) and these design motifs are treated quite differently in Old Bering Sea II (AD 100 to 300), where more emphasis is placed upon curves, sometimes separated into panels and often symmetrically balanced, which achieve stronger, organic forms. In the final Old Bering Sea artistic phase, III (AD

26. Ivory 'winged objects', showing sequence of forms: (top left to bottom right) Okvik style, Old Bering Sea style, Punuk trident style, Late Punuk turreted style. (After Bandi 1969, 76.)

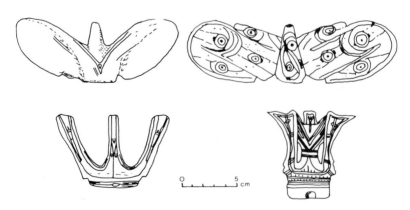

300 to 500), the curves remain firm and are strengthened by circular or eye motifs, and sometimes by raised bosses (fig. 25).

These compelling, ambivalent designs entrance the eye yet tease the imagination: do they represent hunting magic, or the dislocated elements of animals, or mythical sea dwellers and the waves which carry them? The changing forms of the Old Bering Sea engravers are shown very well in the sequence of 'winged objects', perhaps meant either to be attached to the butt end of a harpoon, to act as a flight aid and to counterbalance the heavy harpoon head and socket at the point, or to serve as harpoon rests. These pieces were used by the Okvik hunters, and they appear throughout the Bering Sea tradition (fig. 26).

Punuk developments

Okvik and Old Bering Sea traditions gave way to those of Punuk (AD 500 to 900), much of whose culture was the same, but whose close links with the Siberian mainland are demonstrated by the appearance of sinew-backed bows, wrist guards, bone plate armour, ornaments and tools and, especially, rare pieces of Asian iron, usually made up into engraving tools. The tools influenced the ivory engravers, who now preferred deeply incised, precise lines and mechanically perfect circles, which, in combination, produced a stiff symmetry and angularity well shown in the winged objects, where the early graceful butterflies become sharper and then assume first trident and then, in Late Punuk, turreted forms (fig. 26).

4
The art of the later Alaskan hunters

The spread of the Thule people

By around AD 1000 the way of life specialising in hunting whales, especially the large bowhead whales, which migrate north-eastwards each spring through the narrow ice leads off the Alaskan Arctic coast, had crystallised among the coastal communities, and this very successful approach to making a living is called the Thule culture. Encouraged by access to this important food source, and perhaps by the warmer conditions which developed generally at this time across the northern hemisphere, the Thule people seem to have expanded eastwards across the entire Arctic within a few centuries, although their influence on the Alaskan Pacific coast was diluted, and they never occupied the Aleutian Chain. In the central Arctic and Greenland, their culture is known as Eastern Thule, and it is possible that here Thule people adopted some indigenous ideas, like the building of domed snow houses, which passed back westwards to enrich the repertoire of the Western Thule. From Alaska to eastern Greenland the Thule people maintained a remarkable degree of cultural uniformity and, perhaps, of mutually intelligible language, and they are the ancestors of the modern Inuit (Eskimo).

To hunt the whale and other sea mammals, the Western Thule people used kayaks and umiaks, open skin-covered boats up to 10 metres (33 feet) long, and in the winter they travelled by dog-sled; both umiaks and sleds must have played a crucial role in their expansion. They established permanent coastal winter villages, which each included a number of substantial houses built of whale bones, logs and sods and whose plans encompassed living quarters with elevated benches, storage areas, and entrance passages with cold traps (fig. 27). In the summer, when the group moved to take advantage of the Arctic char, or a similar seasonal food supply, conical skin tents were used. Thule hunting and domestic equipment tends to look more rugged than that of earlier peoples, but it included familiar items — toggle harpoons, with extra-sizes for whale hunting, bird darts, fish spears, men's knives, bow drills and flint flakers. Soapstone was used for lamps and cooking pots, and wood or baleen (the material called 'whalebone' in Europe) for bowls and sleeping mats. Women used ulus with blades of ground slate, skin scrapers, awls, needles

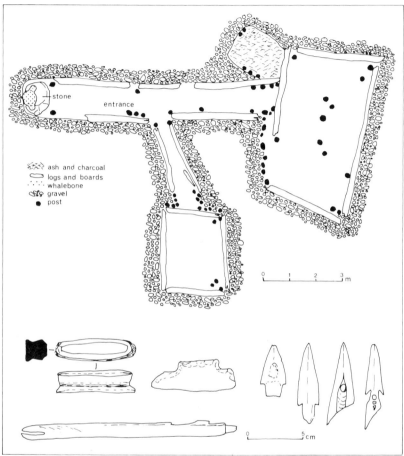

27. Plan of fully developed Thule tradition house (top), Cape Krusenstern, Alaska. Lip ornament, or labret, of coal (middle left). Polished slate ulu (middle centre). Two polished slate projectiles and two ivory harpoon heads (middle right). Antler dart head lacking stone tip (bottom). All from south-west Alaska. (After Dumond 1977, 134, 136.)

(kept in needle cases) and leather thimbles with which to make the all-important fur clothing (fig. 27, 28).

Carving in ivory and wood

The creation of figure sculpture does not seem to have been at the heart of Thule religious life, as it had been for the Okvik or Ipiutak people, although a fine hermaphrodite ivory figurine dating around AD 1200 has been found on St Lawrence Island. However, the later Western Thule people did produce an

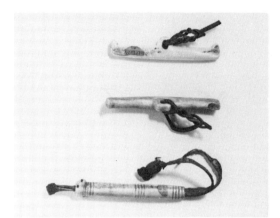

28. Ivory needle case (bottom) to hold fine needles for sewing sealskin, with terminal in the form of a bear's head, and two ivory drag handles for thongs used to pull carcases over the ice; length of needle case 263 millimetres (10⅜ inches). Collected by George Peard, First Lieutenant of His Majesty's Sloop *Blossom* at Kotzebue Sound, north-west Alaska, 1826-7, while the *Blossom* was taking part in the search for Franklin. (Photograph: Exeter City Museum).

inexhaustible variety of vigorous carvings on an enormous range of items of equipment, many of which, now in museum collections, were acquired in the course of voyages of exploration undertaken in the nineteenth century by the Royal Navy, like that of His Majesty's Sloop *Blossom,* which cruised up the Alaskan coast as far north as Kotzebue Sound in 1826-7. Objects like drag handles (figs. 28, 29), for pulling seal carcases, were shaped in the form of sea mammals, and harpoon rests were modelled as two bears, back to back. Arrow straighteners were made in the form of kneeling caribou or decorated with bear heads (fig. 30), and needle cases and other items of sewing equipment took female forms or were enlivened with animal terminals. Ivory tobacco pipes were engraved with lines picked out with black pigment, and carved with rows of seated men or walking bears.

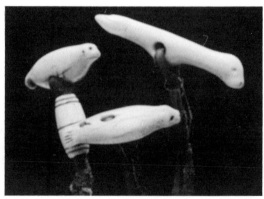

29. Three ivory drag handles in the forms of a sea otter and two seals; length of sea otter 93 millimetres (3⅝ inches). Collected by George Peard at Kotzebue Sound, 1826-7. (Photograph: Exeter City Museum, Bruce Sinclair.)

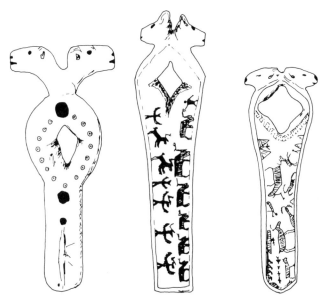

30. Three ivory arrow-shaft straighteners, Western Thule tradition; length of longest, 160 millimetres (6¼ inches). (After Fagg 1972, 21.)

The Bering Sea and Pacific Eskimo were well known for the skilful way in which they carved wooden bowls and containers: food bowls, trays, ladles, and boxes of all kinds. While some of these were carved in one piece, many had separate bottoms and sides, steamed, bent into shape and pegged together into position. Many of the containers were made in the shape of an animal and were embellished with bead and ivory inlays. Some were painted red, and some, especially bowls, had animals, real or mythical, painted in black inside them.

Much of the skin clothing was carefully tailored and decorated with hems and tassels, and a special waterproof coat was made from strips of seal intestine sewn together in horizontal bands. South of the Bering Sea, the men wore wooden visors or conical hunting hats to protect their eyes against the glare. The hats were made of sealskin, or from a single piece of driftwood, scraped thin, bent, and fastened at the back. They were often decorated with paintwork, feathers and flat ivory attachments in the form of walruses and seals. These hats reached their most elaborate forms among the Kodiak Eskimos and the Aleuts, where the decoration included ivory figurines and rows of sea-lion whiskers strung with

31. Three eyeshades. Sealskin with ivory ornaments (left), Alaska; length 215 millimetres (8½ inches). Wood with ivory and feather ornament (centre), Alaska; length 340 millimetres (13⅜ inches). Wood with ivory ornaments (right), Alaska; 275 millimetres (10⅞ inches). (Photograph: British Museum.)

beads and feathers. Aleutian helmets always carried two flat ivory plaques, one on each side, the upper end carved in the form of a scroll, the lower tapering like a bird's beak (fig. 31).

This marvellous range of carving and decoration, although some of it probably had the serious intention of hunting magic, carries an unmistakable sense of humour and *joie de vivre*. Some of the motifs, like the prototypes of some of the objects themselves which appear among the Western Thule, were derived from Ipiutak and Punuk/Old Bering Sea/Okvik forerunners, but the great outburst of carving and decorative work, on all manner of domestic and hunting gear, as far as we can see from the archaeological record, began fairly late in the prehistoric period, and its exuberance presumably reflects a time when a well organised population was in balance with the natural resources.

Pictorial engravings

Among the most charming of the Western Thule pieces are the pictorial engravings on ivory, often on all four sides of bow drills, which show all aspects of Eskimo life (fig. 32). In Alaska in the late eighteenth and nineteenth centuries the creation of these pieces was restricted to the Bering Strait and the adjacent coastal areas from Norton Sound northwards to Kotzebue Sound.

The engravings consist of small silhouettes, often picked out in black, densely organised along the ivory length. They show men in skin boats harpooning whales and walruses, archers shooting caribou, masked men dancing, and men wrestling, running races and, sometimes, fighting with bows and arrows. Often the same ivory portrays a winter village with smoke rising from the roofs, or summer tents, fish racks and food caches raised out of reach of the dogs. Some of the engravings have rhythmical lines of game animals, possibly representing hunting tallies.

These engravings were very popular among the European ships' crews, and they had a considerable vogue after 1848, when the first American whaling vessel passed through the Bering Strait. The ivories showing sailing ships and firearms date from this time, and as the last decades of the nineteenth century progressed the engravings became thicker and heavier, they began to show creatures and landscapes in perspective with delicate shading, and the carvers began to cover whole walrus

32. Both sides of two ivory snow knives (for cutting snow blocks) (above and below). Both sides of two ivory bow drills (centre); length of longest bow drill 413 millimetres (16¼ inches). All are decorated with pictorial engravings. Collected by George Peard at Kotzebue Sound, 1826-7. (Photograph: Exeter City Museum, Bruce Sinclair.)

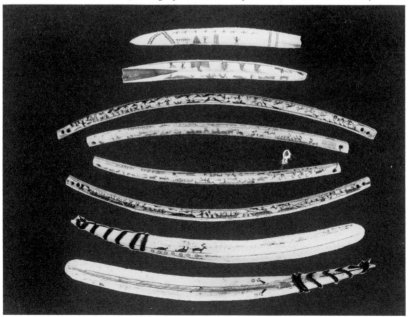

tusks, or to make objects like cribbage boards, to suit the
European taste.

An ivory bodkin with silhouette engraving was found in a
house at Cape Krustenstern dated about AD 1000, and others
excavated from Thule/Punuk sites at Cape Prince of Wales,
north-west Alaska, show that this was a genuinely Eskimo artistic
style which originated in the broad Bering Strait area in
prehistoric times. The Cape Prince of Wales pieces include
representations of four men in an umiak harpooning a whale, and
of two men in kayaks throwing bird spears at a loon, among other
more strictly geometric forms, and this tradition seems to
represent the background from which the later pictorial engraving emerged.

Masks

There is nothing in the archaeological record which suggests
that masks formed a major part of the religious expression of the
early Alaskan people. They are absent from the Okvik, Old
Bering Sea and Punuk sites on St Lawrence Island, where many
kinds of wooden objects were well preserved in the frozen soil,
but parts of three wooden masks have been found at the
Thule-Punuk site of Kurigitavik at Cape Prince of Wales,
showing that they were used, although perhaps rarely, in
prehistoric times. The flowering of mask carving, like that of
Western Thule ivory carving, seems to have been a feature of the
eighteenth and nineteenth centuries and it happened among the
communities around the sweep of the Alaskan coast, from the
Point Hope area in the north to the southern margin of Eskimo
territory at Prince William Sound in the south. The elaborate
masks of the Bering Sea/lower Yukon River and neighbouring
areas represent one of the pinnacles of Eskimo art.

The masks were carved by shamans, or by carvers working
under their directions, and essentially they represent spirits,
usually of animal helpers which the shaman has encountered in
his visits to the spirit world; occasionally the masks may represent
the spirit of places, of ancient objects or of heavenly bodies.
Their purpose was to ward off evil influences and exorcise
malignant spirits which might threaten misfortune to the community, and to appease and honour the souls of the food animals
which the group had killed so that their malice might be averted
and a plentiful supply of meat ensured for the future.

The shaman carvers, therefore, had to draw on their imagina-
tions to produce plastic forms which, although recognisably

human or animal, reflected the awe-inspiring, bizarre and terrible spirit-creatures which they alone had access to and could control. For this reason many of the masks, especially those of the Bering Sea area, are highly grotesque, with surrealistic combinations of eyes and faces, animal and human forms superimposed, and every conceivable distortion of mouth, face and head.

The Bering Sea masks are the most elaborate, not only in their complex designs, but also in their appendages. Narrow hoops of wood or willow often encircled the face, and attached to these, or to the face itself, were feathers, wooden figurines of birds, animals and human limbs, or fringes of caribou hair. Some masks had movable doors which would open to show the soul of the animal represented in the outer carving, or a human face inside the animal mask, illustrating the conviction of close kinship between men and creatures and the belief that animals encountered in the wild might push up their own muzzles to reveal their human faces. Bering Sea masks were usually painted, either in white or soft shades of blue, green and grey, or with areas of

33. Softwood mask painted red, white, pink, blue and black; length 300 millimetres (11⅞ inches). Probably Prince William Sound, western Alaska. (Photograph: British Museum.)

bolder black or red accentuating special areas or features.

By contrast, the masks of the northern Eskimo were less elaborate. Some of the Point Hope pieces are portrait-like, and others are restrained and abstract, often in bold relief carving. They are more simply painted and lack dangling appendages. In the south, around Prince William Sound, the masks feature wedge-shaped noses, high foreheads, heavily emphasised eyebrows and simple decoration (fig. 33). Masks were also created on Kodiak Island and in the Aleutian Islands.

The masks were worn by male dancers in the winter feasts, such as the Messenger Feast, honouring dead animals, and the Bladder Festival, propitiating animals yet to be hunted. These ceremonies went on for days and included dances, in which the men jumped and stamped vigorously in time to the singing and the beat of the single-sided drum, mask wearing, and the use of purifying smoke. Women held finger masks, small wooden discs with finger holes, decorated with feathers, and moved their arms and upper bodies rhythmically to the accompaniment of the music. The Bering Sea Eskimos were still holding these mask festivals in the 1870s.

34. Five human figurines in ivory and bone; height of largest 199 millimetres (7⅞ inches). All probably Thule culture and from central or eastern Arctic. (Photograph: Robert and Lisa Sainsbury Collection, University of East Anglia.)

5
The Eastern Thule people

Eastern Thule settlers

The modern Eskimo of Igloolik, and indeed many of the people of the central Arctic, tell stories of the Tunit people, who were good caribou hunters and also caught seals and walruses. Finally, the Igloolik Eskimo say, their ancestors drove out the Tunit after several battles and took possession of the land. The Tunit are associated with definite places, and these are usually abandoned settlements of the Dorset people. The legend seems to be an orally transmitted reflection of the disappearance about AD 1000 of Dorset traditions, which by then had dominated the area for around two thousand years, when confronted by the whale-hunting Thule people, who expanded rapidly from Alaska across the Arctic at that time.

An important reason for this may have been the warmer conditions of the time, which cut down the pack-ice and enabled the whales and other sea mammals to move more freely in their annual migrations. The hunters were forced to adopt open-sea tactics, which involved a pursuit in open water by one umiak accompanied by a fleet of kayaks. Once this technique had been perfected, it could be used to follow the whales to their summer feeding grounds around the Beaufort Sea and the Arctic islands, so creating the spread of people which the archaeology shows. The taking of a single whale would be enough to provide food for a whole winter for the number of men required to stalk and kill it, and for their families, and many villages may simply mark the spot where a whale was killed. The hunting method also made the captain of the umiak a very important man.

Along the central Arctic and Greenland coasts the Thule people established their permanent winter villages, built of turf, stone and whalebone, smaller than those in Alaska and perhaps occupied for shorter lengths of time. They adapted their hunting methods to local animals and conditions, and they perhaps learnt some Dorest traditions, which were passed back to the Alaskan homeland. The same warmer conditions had attracted Norse settlers to Southern Greenland, and Eskimo and Europeans were encountering each other along the Greenland coasts from about AD 1200.

Eastern Thule carvers

The art of the Eastern Thule, like their technology, is largely based upon Alaskan traditions and appears thin by comparison with that of their Dorset predecessors, although the Western Thule ivory figures already noted (see chapter 4) and the wealth of material from Angmagssalik (see below) show the capabilities of Thule carvers. Nevertheless, most of the figurines recovered from Eastern Thule sites consist of simple figures in wood or ivory, showing men or women with flat, unmarked faces and short, stumpy arms; these may have been children's dolls or amulets (fig. 34). Small ivory birds, or birds with women's heads, are another common form. They are carved with flat bases so that they resemble seabirds sitting on the water, and these may have been used as pieces in a hand game. Occasional toggles and other small pieces are carved with human or animal heads (fig. 35) and there are also a few small whale representations.

The Thule people were, however, very interested in adding engraved designs to their artefacts, particularly to objects of ivory, especially either weapons used in hunting the sea mammals, or needle cases, combs, decorative chains with spherical or elongated bodkin-like terminals and pendants, all particularly associated with women. Many of these pieces carry single or double marginal lines, sometimes connected with cross-hatching, Y designs and matchstick-figure men. Occasionally these techniques flower into full-blown decorative panels showing hunting or camp scenes, like that on a late Thule ivory bow drill recovered from a grave near Arctic Bay, on north-west Baffin Island (fig. 36). Finds like this are important because they demonstrate that

35. Two ivory combs, probably Thule culture and from central or eastern Arctic; height of largest 75 millimetres (3 inches). (Photograph: Robert and Lisa Sainsbury Collection, University of East Anglia.)

36. Ivory bow drill, late Thule tradition, Arctic Bay, north-west Baffin Island; length 440 millimetres (17⅜ inches). On the left a battle seems to be taking place in front of summer tents; on the right people stand before tents and others paddle out in kayaks to hunt a swimming caribou. (After Dumond 1977, 142-3.)

this pictorial art is a genuine element in the artistic repertoire of the Eastern Thule people as well as that of their cousins in western Alaska.

Robert McGhee has argued that the use of ivory in the manufacture of this range of hunting, sewing and ornamental or amulet material, and perhaps its associated decoration, reflects the Thule view of the world, as we can perceive it dimly through the mythology and religion of their historic and present-day descendants. The Thule universe may have been based on a set of contrasts between, on the one hand, things associated with women, the sea, sea-mammal hunting and perhaps winter life, and, on the other hand, things associated with men, land animals and summer life on the land. So, most Thule sealing and whaling harpoon heads are made from ivory or sea-mammal bone, while arrowheads used for hunting caribou in summer are made from caribou antler.

This tension between opposites generates vital energy among the Arctic people, as it does among most people, and ivory, the most precious material known in the far north, is reserved for the female side of life, although the male carvers who work it and the male hunters who kill with it participate in it. So do the shamans, whose lifestyles sometimes embrace female elements and who can pass into various states of being: obvious shamanistic gear is not conspicuous in the Thule archaeological record but European accounts of historic Eskimo religion suggests that they played an important role.

The art of Angmagssalik

Gustav Holm reached the isolated settlement of Angmagssalik, on the east coast of Greenland in 1884, the first European to do so, and he found there an artistic achievement which rivalled that of the contemporary Alaskans, demonstrating yet again the inherent talent of the Eskimo, which will find expression in appropriate circumstances. At Angmagssalik, the stimulus to creation seems to have been a dark one: the villagers told Holm that there had been a disastrous decline in the number of seals over the last generation, the fishing had grown poor, and many had died of starvation, while murders had become frequent and blood feuds disrupted the community.

Archaeology has demonstrated that the culture of the east Greenland Eskimo was Thule, but perhaps much influenced by underlying and ancient Dorset traditions. The art of the Angmagssalik carvers drew on this rich inheritance, but it seems clear that a distinct artistic revival happened about 1850, perhaps in response to worsening conditions. It is not surprising that the main purpose of the carvings seems to be protection, to ward off evil spirits and to make the spirits yield up the hunters' catch.

Driftwood was freely available, and wooden figurines were frequently carved, often depicting bears and bear hunters, and clearly intended to conjure up bears for food. Wooden figurines of women, of a standard pattern with heavy thighs and breasts and rectangular top-knots, were frequently carved. These combine the massive figure solidity of Dorset sculptures with the simplified stylisation of Thule traditions, but their purpose, magical or otherwise, is not known. Many implements, like water buckets, scoops, boxes, eyeshades and harpoon throwers, were made of wood, and on to these were riveted small, flat, ivory representations of seals and other sea mammals, stylised to a greater or lesser degree, to give relief decoration of rich, almost rococo effect, doubtless also intended to encourage the seal towards the hunter's harpoon (fig. 37).

Masks showing human faces were also carved in wood, characteristically showing deep horizontal lines which probably represent tattoo marks; the surfaces were usually polished black so that the lines stood out more clearly. These masks represent the shaman's helping spirits, creatures part human, part sea mammal (fig. 38). Life at Angmagssalik was so dominated by the fear of evil that hunters also had their helping spirits, known as *tupilaks,* creatures barely controlled by the hunter himself, and of ill omen to the rest of the community. These often terrifying concepts, like that represented by a figure half raven, half dead child (fig. 39), embody the tension and despair of the community.

Artistic decline
The dramatic decline documented at Angmagssalik seems to

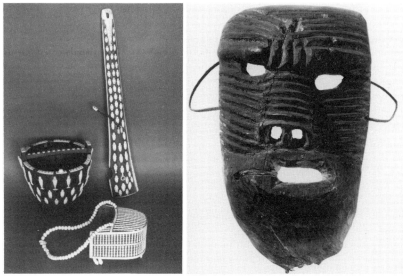

37. *(above left)* Bucket, eyeshade with bead-strung thong, and spear-thrower, all of wood with bone or ivory applied decoration; length of spear-thrower 630 millimetres (24¾ inches). Angmagssalik, eastern Greenland. (Photograph: British Museum.)

38. *(above right)* Wooden mask with grooved and blackened surface; height 265 millimetres (10½ inches). Angmagssalik, eastern Greenland. (Photograph: British Museum.)

39. *(below)* Wooden figure of a *tupilak,* an evil spirit, half raven, half dead child; length 120 millimetres (4¾ inches). Angmagssalik, eastern Greenland. (Photograph: British Museum.)

have been the fate of most of the Thule communities in the central and eastern Arctic. Archaeology shows that around AD 1500 their winter villages, well built, well supplied with stored food and representing a secure, prosperous lifestyle, were scattered across the Arctic, but European accounts demonstrate that by about 1800-30 much of the region was unoccupied and elsewhere people were living the precarious life of small shifting bands, occupying skin tents in the summer and temporary snow houses in winter.

A major factor in this decline seems to have been the onset about AD 1600 of harsher conditions, which affected the whole of the northern hemisphere. In the Arctic, the shorter summers and the increased amounts of pack-ice and solid ice altered the numbers and the habits of the sea mammals so that the vital summer hunting suffered. In the far north, the Eskimo communities reacted by abandoning the High Arctic almost completely. Further south, hunting groups began to turn inland to the caribou and the lake and river fishing, so that kayaks were adapted to river use, while umiaks and whale-hunting techniques were less useful and became obsolete, together with the community enterprise which they had embodied. The new life could not accumulate enough food to last the winter in a permanent village, so the seal in areas of winter ice had to be hunted to extinction, and a new area found for the next year. All this may have led to a population decline, and increasing contact with European technology may have sapped traditional skills and values. As an inevitable result of diminishing vitality and confidence, most Eskimo communities ceased to produce decorative or plastic art.

40. Soapstone figurine of a seal, carved in 1974 by Isaccie, Frobisher Bay, Baffin Island, with its guarantee tag; length 163 millimetres (6⅜ inches). (Photograph: Bruce Sinclair.)

6
Modern Eskimo sculptors

The European impact after 1945

By the end of the Second World War, throughout the Canadian Arctic the old hunting economy had largely collapsed and its place had been taken by the miserable conditions which always seem to succeed the erosion of a traditional way of life. Hunting rifles, provided by white traders, had diminished the wildlife reserves. Disease had become a ferocious problem, and the earlier ravages of measles and chicken pox had been followed by tuberculosis. Child mortality was high, alcoholism was on the increase, and general life expectancy was around forty years. More and more, people were becoming dependent upon store-bought goods, for the purchase of which they had no regular cash wage. At root, all these factors were symptoms rather than causes and sprang from the disintergration of human personalities deprived of their traditional framework.

Conditions were perhaps better among the Eskimo of Alaska, where opportunities for employment were greater, and were certainly better among the southern Greenland Eskimo, where, especially in the kinder fjord valleys below the ice-cap, the Danish government has encouraged the development of farming. Communities like Igaliko in south-west Greenland, on the site of the twelfth-century cathedral of St Nicholas, and not far from the site of Erik the Red's farmstead, show how, here, viable prosperity and human dignity can be combined. Such comparatively comfortable solutions are impossible further north.

By 1950 the Canadian government, upon which the brunt of the problem fell, had begun to be acutely conscious of, and conscience-stricken over, the human misery in its Northwest Territories, in a world increasingly aware of the legacy of colonialism. Tender conscience apart, there were two other compelling reasons for governmental intervention in the north. The Arctic Ocean is an element in the strategic thinking of the Western powers and large military installations have been developed at Alert, on the northern tip of Ellesmere Island, and elsewhere. Equally, the mineral wealth of the Arctic is truly vast. Oil and gas deposits exist in the Mackenzie Valley and on the Alaskan North Slope, where they are being tapped by the enormous British Petroleum and Standard Oil Company (Ohio) plant based on Prudhoe Bay (fig. 3); further deposits are being explored in north Arctic islands. The ancient rocks of the Canadian Shield, which covers much of the continental Barren Grounds and extends into the southern Arctic islands, contain a huge range of metals and other minerals.

Faced with the twin facts of accelerating exploitation and the decay of native society, the Canadian government, through its Department of Indian and Northern Affairs, has developed a massive welfare programme aimed at bringing the basic services of education, health care, radio communication, air transport and social security to the north. It has also encouraged the trading co-operatives, which market local products. This has necessitated the creation of some thirty settlements throughout the north, like those at Igloolik or Arctic Bay, where most of the population is now fixed, living permanently in the wooden prefabricated houses supplied by the government, travelling by air to visit friends, or locally on the mechanised sledges known as skidoos. It is easy to criticise and to be regretful because something unique has gone from the earth, but lamentations will not help the modern Eskimo to come to terms with the intrusive world, in which, it is to be hoped, some of their traditional values and virtues may survive.

The genesis of modern Eskimo art

These developments are the context of the outburst of modern Eskimo art, which was brought into being, almost single-handedly, by James Houston. In 1948 Houston, himself an artist, visited Eskimo settlements on the eastern side of Hudson Bay. He saw for himself how desperately they needed a livelihood, and he encouraged the people of Inoucdjouac, Cape Smith and Povungnituk to make more of the soapstone carving which, at that time, was confined to the production of seal-oil lamps and pots. Houston was surprised at the quality of the small animal, bird and human figurines which he collected. In 1948 several hundred were exhibited by the Canadian Handicrafts Guild in Montreal and sold very rapidly.

The potential was obvious, and through Houston's efforts art centres were established, not only on the east Hudson Bay coast, but also at Cape Dorset, Lake Harbour and Repulse Bay, among others. In the 1950s a print studio was organised at Cape Dorset, and print collections are now formed annually here and at Baker Lake, Holman Island and Pangnirtung. Most of the Eskimo

41. Underside of seal figurine shown in figure 40, showing carver's name, Isaccie (e-sah-ke), in Eskimo syllabics. (Photograph: Bruce Sinclair.)

settlements now have workshops, supported by Eskimo-run co-operatives and with transport assistance provided by the Hudson Bay Company.

Eskimo art is marketed in the south through Canadian Arctic Producers (CAP), a private company set up with government backing, which acts as wholesaler. Genuine pieces usually carry the igloo official trademark, and sometimes the artist has also scratched his or her signature on the base of the carving, either in Roman script or Eskimo syllabics (a script designed to cope with the many-syllabled Eskimo words) (fig. 41). Print workshops, also, have adopted their own symbols (fig. 42). These marks are intended to distinguish authentic products from the many fakes now on the market. In 1967 the Canadian Eskimo Arts Council was formed so that advice could be offered on matters of artistic development and quality. In 1970 the Council organised the exhibition 'Sculpture of the Inuit : Master Works of the Canadian Arctic', which toured the major western museums for three years and, really for the first time, displayed the Eskimo artistic heritage to the world.

The principal modern schools

The most important centres of the modern artistic movement are concentrated around the shores of Foxe Basin and across on the eastern Baffin coast, and on the northern shores of Hudson Bay, a distribution which broadly follows that of the earlier Dorset culture.

On the west coast of Hudson Bay, the settlements at both Rankin Inlet and Baker Lake have made important contributions. Kavik, the doyen of Rankin Inlet, has specialised in figure forms, poised between the naturalistic and the abstract, and his younger contemporary Arlook has extended this abstraction of forms. At Baker Lake, carvers like Akkanashoonak have created massive human and animal sculptures, while Seeroga, another

42. *(left)* Identification marks of print workshops. Ivujivik, Wakeham Bay (above). Baker Lake, Inoucdjouac (centre). Cape Dorset, Holman Island (below).
43. *(right)* Soapstone figurine *Man with Fish in Snow Crevice,* carved in 1972 by Selasie, Povungnituk, Hudson Bay; length 165 millimetres (6½ inches). (Photograph: Exeter City Museum, Bruce Sinclair.)

important carver from the same settlement, creates dream-like figures in stone and in prints. On the east coast, the settlements of Povungnituk and Inoucdjouac have produced notable work (fig. 43).

All the carvers mentioned so far work in soapstone, easily cut with a knife when it is wet. At the south-eastern tip of the eastern Hudson Bay coast, however, there are deposits of very beautiful argillite, dark green with veins of lighter or darker colour showing on revealed surfaces. This is harder than soapstone and lends itself to smoother, stronger lines, qualities that appeal to the carvers of the Belcher Islands, like Sam Willie Ekalok, and of the Great Whale River, like Davidee Kagvik, who is noted for his lyrical figure forms.

Cape Dorset, the ancient centre in south-west Baffin Island, produced the most prestigious of the early contemporary Eskimo sculptors, and among their work pieces like *Spirit,* a greenstone figure part bear, part fish and with a human face, carved by Kabubawakota, stand out as major achievements in the whole history of Eskimo art (fig. 44). The best of the Cape Dorset animal-spirit figures have indeed a dream-like, mystical force, uniquely Eskimo but also universal. On the eastern side of Baffin Island, the carvers of Frobisher Bay and of Lake Harbour make use of nearby deposits of light green, hard serpentine, as well as soapstone. Carvers like Kootoo shape bird and seal figurines, abstract and yet drawn from a lifetime of intimate observation. Further north, the settlement of Pangnirtung is recognised as the most important centre of whalebone carving, the result, chiefly, of the influential work of Keeokjuk, in whose hands the anatomical forms of whale ribs or vertebrae fuse into the shape of the finished carving.

The famous centres and their prized carvers are supported by a great depth of creative activity which is widespread among all the settlements of Arctic Canada and is beginning to appear among their fellows in Alaska and, to a more limited extent, in Greenland. In settlements like Igloolik or Frobisher Bay the visitor will be offered small carvings produced by virtually all members of the community (fig. 45). These may not achieve any great heights of expression, but they are genuine of their kind, and they keep alive the spirit of practice and experiment.

44. Green soapstone figure *Spirit*, carved by Kabubawakota, Cape Dorset, central Arctic; height 413 millimetres (16¼ inches). (Photograph: Montreal Museum of Fine Arts.)

Quality of modern Eskimo art

Since about 1950 people outside the Arctic have become aware of the Eskimo artistic tradition and have had to come to terms with its claims to be one of the great aesthetic traditions of the world. Most of the western capitals have experienced major exhibitions of Eskimo art, several finely illustrated books have been produced, and leading dealers have assembled impressive collections for sale. Although many of these ventures have looked backwards to the carving of the times before European contact, they tend to concentrate upon modern work, particularly if works are being offered for sale to the public.

This has resulted in the creation of a large North American and Western European market for Eskimo pieces, many of which can be purchased relatively cheaply and chosen from an increasing range which includes not only carvings in stone and bone and prints, but also basketwork, jewellery and assorted knick-knacks constructed from oddments of fur and bone. The deliberately stimulated demand creates a backlash in the Eskimo communities, where sales of locally made handicrafts have become economically increasingly important.

The central dilemma facing contemporary Eskimo artists and their advisers is, inevitably, that facing every school of craftsmen: is it possible to combine a viable level of sales with a genuine respect for the integrity of the work and the traditions of the past?

45. Carver roughing out a carving from the raw stone block, Frobisher Bay (?), Baffin Island. (Photograph: Canadian Government Photo Centre.)

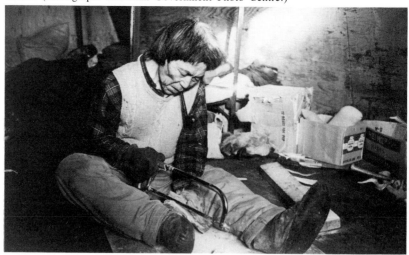

Even leaving out of account the smaller models, toys and copies as not worth discussing, and concentrating upon the more prestigious stone and bone carvings and prints, we have to feel a certain unease.

A carving guaranteed by one of the organising bodies is made from genuine whalebone or stone, was made in the Arctic by an Eskimo carver and was produced by hand, with (usually) the simplest of hand tools. It is, in other words, an authentic piece of craftsmanship. Its aesthetic qualities are another matter. Some contemporary carvings, and these not the least prized by many western connoisseurs, reflect in their contrasted forms the dreams and nightmares of disturbance, either of minds unbalanced by conflicting pressures or of ancient memories of shamanistic vision. More accessible to western feeling, but drawing in their design equally upon the Eskimo heritage, are the animal carvings, usually of birds, seals, walruses and polar bears. At their best these embody great power, and almost all of them capture in their clean lines, and often with humour, the pleasure of the living creature. There remains the very large range of human realistic figure carvings, depicting hunters, children, women with babies in their hoods and similar life scenes. These themes are a new departure, sometimes strong but often sentimentalised and trivialised to match the demands of western buyers.

The moral and artistic problems which the deliberate encouragement of 'native art', like that of the Eskimo, engenders are legion, and they seem to be essentially insoluble, certainly now, and perhaps always. The exploitive element is easy to pick out and condemn: the western buyers who pay for poor designs, probably in the belief that they are acquiring quality goods, and the carvers who are reduced to producing routine, shoddily imagined pieces by the demands of the market. In the end, perhaps, none of this matters as much as we sometimes think. All artistic movements have their poor underside, and most produce much which is best forgotten. In the contemporary Eskimo artistic outburst, as always, the memorable pieces, like Kabubawakota's *Spirit,* will remain, and for these we should be grateful. The whole of their history shows that the creative talents of the Eskimo people are vigorous enough to ensure that their artistic tradition will survive and flourish.

7
Museums to visit

The following museums have collections of Eskimo art:

United Kingdom

Museum of Mankind (the Ethnography Department of the British Museum), 6 Burlington Gardens, London W1X 2EX. Telephone: 01-437 2224 or 2228.

Pitt Rivers Museum, South Parks Road, Oxford OX1 3PP. Telephone: Oxford (0865) 512541.

Royal Albert Memorial Museum, Queen Street, Exeter, Devon EX4 3RX. Telephone: Exeter (0392) 56724.

University Museum of Archaeology and Anthropology, Downing Street, Cambridge CB2 3DZ. Telephone: Cambridge (0223) 359714.

Canada

Eskimo Museum, 242 La Verendyre Street, Churchill, Manitoba R0B 0E0.

National Museum of Man, Victoria Memorial Museum Building, McLeod at Metcalfe, Ottawa, Ontario K1A 0M8.

Denmark

Danish National Museum, Ny Vestergade 10, Copenhagen K.

Union of Soviet Socialist Republics

Leningrad Anthropological and Ethnographical Museum, Universitetskaya Naberezhnayo 3, Leningrad B-164.

United States of America

Alaska State Museum, Subport, Pouch FM, Juneau, Alaska 99811.

American Museum of Natural History, 79th Street and Central Park West, New York, NY 10024.

Anchorage Historical and Fine Arts Museum, 121 West Seventh Avenue, Anchorage, Alaska 99501.

Smithsonian Institution, 1000 Jefferson Drive SW, Washington DC 20560.

University of Alaska Museum, University of Alaska, Fairbanks, Alaska 99701.